ALIENS ™

publisher **Mike Richardson**

series editors **Ryder Windham and Anina Bennett**
collection editor **Suzanne Taylor**
collection designer **Amy Arendts**
book design manager **Brian Gogolin**

special thanks to **Maury McIntyre at Twentieth Century Fox**
Steve Perry • **Den Beauvais** and **Monty Sheldon**

inspired by **the original Alien designs of H.R. Giger**

**Published by
Titan Books Ltd.
42-44 Dolben Street
London SE1 0UP**

**First edition: September 1997
ISBN: 1-85286-851-1**

1 2 3 4 5 6 7 8 9 10

Printed in Canada

ALIENS
ROGUE

script **Ian Edginton**

art **Will Simpson**

colors **Robbie Busch**

cover **John Bolton**

lettering **John Costanza**

TITAN BOOKS

We Remember When...

There are some events where people just remember what they were doing at the time. Or who they were with.

Moon landings, deaths of important people, the first kiss. And for many people like us, movies. But only certain movies. Important movies.

Dean's top three movies of memory are *Wait Until Dark*, *MASH*, and *Alien*. For Kris the movies are *The Wizard of Oz*, *Star Wars*, and *Alien*. And for both of us together, *Aliens*.

Aliens was the first movie we saw as a couple, so of course we're going to remember it.

As you might be able to tell, the *Aliens* series was very important to both of us. Now, at the moment we won't go into why *MASH* was important to Dean, or how *Star Wars* got Kris going more toward science fiction, and how she has now actually written one of the *Star Wars* hardbacks called *The New Rebellion*.

But let us tell you about that first *Aliens* movie together in Madison, Wisconsin. We'd known each other for only a few weeks, and we both had been hesitant to tell the other that we really, really wanted to see the new *Aliens*. Finally, we communicated, and one very hot, sticky night we picked an early show, grabbed our popcorn money, and headed for the wonderfully cool air conditioning of the theater. Dean thinks the theater was a six-plex. Kris says four-plex. But such is the memory of a couple after a decade of being together.

Now, at that early stage of the relationship, Dean had not yet realized Kris got into movies. No, a better way to describe it would be Kris got inside movies. In other words, she lived them during the two-plus hours the film was rolling. And because Dean didn't know that, he made one major mistake at that first movie experience — he let Kris hold the popcorn.

Before that large tub was half eaten, it suddenly became airborne. Kris, being inside the movie, had reacted to a specifically frightening moment in the movie, of which in *Aliens* there are a number. Her arm jerked upward and with it the popcorn.

The tub stayed in her hand, empty, and the popcorn almost reached orbit. Or so it seemed in the slow motion of the moment.

But like NASA discovered, what goes up must come down. As luck would have it, the popcorn did not land on Dean, but on a family two rows back, who seemed, between the screams of terror at the movie, to understand. They were also long gone by the time we emerged from the end of that movie.

At the time, both of us were fledgling writers, both having sold short stories and written a few novels. We talked a great deal about that movie that night, trying to figure out, as writers do, what made it work.

Then it went the way of other first movies: into the world of pleasant memory. Of course, Dean still never lets Kris hold the popcorn.

Jump ahead a few years to 1993.

Kris and Dean are now full-time fiction writers. Kris is editing part-time the *Magazine of Fantasy and Science Fiction* and Dean is editing *Pulphouse Magazine*. During this period, we just happened to attend a local Oregon convention where we met our friend and great writer, Steve Perry. At that time he was the author of the new *Aliens* novels that were popping up on newsstands all over the country. Now, Kris and Dean were both very envious of Steve getting to work on *Aliens*. And if Dean remembers right, we told Steve so about a dozen times each.

So he told us to quit bowing at his feet and go write one of our own.

We, of course, asked the master how, and he pointed to a woman across the convention hallway. As it worked out, it was another friend of ours who had just been hired by Dark Horse to do book editing.

Dean has a memory of climbing over a restaurant booth to get to her, but Kris feels that might be a fiction writer's imagination going just a little too far. Let's just say that we told her our movie and popcorn story, then told her how much we loved the Dark Horse comics and how much we loved Steve Perry's books and then about our love for the movies. And the characters. And the art. Everything. We loved everything about the *Aliens* books.

In other words, we groveled.

She checked with her boss, and the fine folks at Bantam Books, and then she called us and said yes. Most likely just to get us off her back. But she did say yes, and that was what was important. We were getting a dream come true. We were getting to work in the *Aliens* universe.

So just like the first movie (except we didn't hold hands and no popcorn got over ten feet in the air) we wrote the novel *Aliens: Rogue* together under the name Sandy Schofield. It was great fun taking the wonderful Dark Horse series, written by Ian Edginton and drawn by Will Simpson, and adapting it into prose. It was like the first movie date all over again. One of those writing experiences we will always remember. Just like the movie.

Between us we've now written over forty novels, and we're still very proud of *Aliens: Rogue*. Which is saying something after all this time.

And now we get to introduce the *Aliens: Rogue* trade-paperback edition of the comics. It seems as if things have now come full circle. And that feels right.

The only thing that would be better is if they ask us to do another *Aliens* novel.

Hint. Hint.

Grovel. Grovel.

Dean Wesley Smith
& Kristine Kathryn Rusch
writing as Sandy Schofield
Lincoln City, Oregon 1997

Detail from Will Simpson's cover art for issue #3 of the *Aliens: Rogue* comic-book series.

"AS MUCH AS WE HAVE COME TO FEAR THE ALIEN, IT CANNOT BE DENIED THAT IT HAS HAD A PROFOUND EFFECT ON OUR CULTURE.

"TECHNOLOGIES DESIGNED TO COMBAT IT HAVE BECOME ASSIMILATED SEAMLESSLY INTO THE MOST DOMESTIC OF OUR ENVIRONMENTS.

"DRUGS PROCESSED FROM THE ALIEN MATRIARCH'S ROYAL JELLY ARE NOW AVAILABLE COMMERCIALLY.

"NEW ECONOMIES BUILT ON THE BACK OF A CREATURE THAT USED US AS BREEDING STOCK.

"IT'S A UNIQUE INDICTMENT OF THE HUMAN CONDITION -- WE DON'T JUST CONQUER OUR FEARS, WE MARKET THEM.

"BUT IN DOING SO WE'VE LOST SIGHT OF SOMETHING..."

"...WE'VE FORGOTTEN THAT WE WERE ONCE PREY, NOT PREDATOR-- FORGOTTEN THE INTENSE TERROR, THE CLAUSTROPHOBIC HORROR..."

"...THE ALIENATION..."

OKAY, HERE'S THE DRILL: WE'RE AFTER A MATURE WARRIOR-- INTACT. I KNOW IT STINKS, BUT THAT'S THE JOB.

I WANT TASER-WEBS ONLY. FIREARMS SLUNG UNLESS ON MY ORDER, UNDERSTOOD?

YES, SIR.

LET'S GET TO IT. McPHILLIPS, TAKE POINT.

SIGNAL'S CLEAN. NO MOVEMENT.

KEEP IT TIGHT, PEOPLE-- CHECK THOSE CORNERS...

...AND WATCH THE WALLS. WE ALL KNOW THEIR GAME PLAN.

DON'T LET THEM GET BEHIND--

"WE JUST GAVE 'EM AN ALARM CALL...

"...AND NOW THEY'RE COMIN' DOWN TO BREAKFAST."

COMBAT SPACING FRONT AND REAR! HUSTLE! HUSTLE! DILLON-- THE CANNON?

PREPPED AND READY, SIR. MAX FREQUENCY, WIDE FIELD FOCUS.

STAND BY, TASER WEBS...

...'CAUSE HERE THEY COME! DILLON, FIRE ON MY MARK.

NOW!

HHHSSSSSS

THE GUN STIRS LIGHTLY IN HIS HANDS--NO SOUND, NO FIREFLASH, NO RECOIL. JUST A FAINT *SHIMMER* IN THE AIR...

BUT NEVER ENOUGH.

GOTTA SHUT IT OFF OR SHE'LL BLOW!

CRITICAL POWER OVERLOAD 22:09 SEC.

SERGEANT REUBEN GREEN IS A THIRTY-YEAR MAN, LIKE HIS FATHER AND HIS FATHER BEFORE HIM.

A BLOODLINE OF *WARRIORS* BRED ON CONFLICT AND GLORY, HONOR AND SACRIFICE.

AN ANCIENT PROFESSION.

TIMES CHANGE.

COMPANIES REPLACE COUNTRIES.

THE FLAG GIVES WAY TO A *DOLLAR BILL.*

AN AGE-OLD PROFESSION IS SWEPT ASIDE...

...BY THE SHOCK OF THE NEW.

SPACE--THE FORGE OF CREATION, THE LATHE OF HEAVEN.

THERE ARE A THOUSAND WAYS TO DIE OUT HERE. A THOUSAND WAYS TO LET THE HUNGRY VACUUM TEAR AWAY YOUR LIFE.

YET WE CONTINUE TO HURL OURSELVES INTO THE VOID. WRAPPED IN SHELLS OF PLASTIC AND METAL, WE CHALLENGE THE PREDATORY EMPTINESS WITH OUR MERE EXISTENCE.

WITH INTELLECT AND ARROGANCE WE CONFRONT THE DARKNESS. AFTER ALL, WE ARE NATURE'S CHILDREN...

... AND NATURE ABHORS A VACUUM.

CHARON BASE FLIGHT CONTROL. THIS IS ZAJER/COMM TECHNIC TRANSPORT VESSEL *CALIBAN*, REG # 19095774, REQUESTING LANDING CLEARANCE, OVER.

ROGER, *CALIBAN*. HANGAR TWELVE'S CLEAR AND READY TO RECEIVE YOU, OVER.

WE'RE IN THE TUBE, NOMINAL TO PROFILE. CUTTING THRUSTERS.

ALL RIGHT, LET'S TUCK HER IN. AND DEEGAN...

YES, BOSS?

WATCH THOSE *CORNERS* THIS TIME, HUH?

HEY, TRUST ME! IT'S A WALK IN THE PARK.

DEEGAN, WHEN DID YOU LAST SEE SOMEONE TAKE EIGHTY THOUSAND UGLY TONS OF METAL FOR A STROLL?

HANGAR TWELVE DECOMPRESSING. ALL CREW AND PASSENGERS, PLEASE REPORT TO DECONTAMINATION.

SO, MR. KRAY, WHAT BRINGS YOU TO SCENIC CHARON?

APART FROM US THAT IS.

CAN IT, DEEGAN-- I'M TALKING TO A NORMAL HUMAN BEING HERE.

THANKS FOR YOUR INTEREST, BUT IT'S CLASSIFIED ON A *NEED-TO-KNOW* BASIS. SORRY.

AND WE DON'T NEED TO KNOW?

GOT IT IN ONE.

FIGURES. KLEIST'S GOT THIS PLACE SEWN UP TIGHTER THAN A FROG'S BUTT.

MR. KRAY?

SPEAK OF THE DEVIL...

...AND HE SHALL APPEAR.

WELCOME TO CHARON. I'M PROFESSOR ERNST KLEIST, DIRECTOR OF THIS FACILITY.

I TRUST YOU HAD A COMFORTABLE FLIGHT?

YES, THANK YOU.

EYES ONLY:
PROFESSOR E. KLEIST
FROM G. DE SOUZA:
CONTROLLER—
RESEARCH AND DEVELOPMENT

HELLO, ERNST. HOW ARE YOU KEEPING? I'M SORRY ABOUT ALL OF THIS CLOAK-AND-DAGGER BUSINESS, BUT WE HAVE SOMETHING OF A SITUATION HERE AND I FELT YOU SHOULD BE BROUGHT UP TO SPEED ON CURRENT EVENTS.

AS YOU MAY ALREADY KNOW, YOUR WORK ON *PROJECT CHIMERA* IS GARNERING UNHEALTHY ATTENTION FROM CERTAIN QUARTERS...

...INCLUDING A NEW ASIAN-CHINESE CONSORTIUM THAT'S ATTEMPTED TO INFILTRATE Z.C.T. ON SEVERAL OCCASIONS.

ALL FUTILE EFFORTS-- UNTIL NOW.

WHEN I RECEIVED YOUR LAST PROJECT UPDATE, THE TRANSMISSION HAD BEEN INTERCEPTED AND DECODED.

A TIDY JOB, BUT CLOSE INVESTIGATION SHOWED THE DATA HAD NOT ONLY BEEN ALTERED BUT WAS INFESTED WITH *VIRAL TIMEBOMBS.*

POINT IS, WE CAN'T BE SURE IF THIS'S THE *FIRST* TIME THEY'VE CRACKED OUR TRANSMISSIONS OR THE *HUNDREDTH!*

WE'RE HAVING TO DEEP-CLEAN ALL OUR SYSTEMS. IT'S A NIGHTMARE, AS YOU CAN IMAGINE.

THE BOTTOM LINE IS THIS: CHIMERA'S OUR HIGHEST PRIORITY. AS OF NOW, YOU ARE TO CEASE ALL TRANSMISSIONS TO EARTH UNTIL FURTHER NOTICE.

WE CAN'T RELY ON OUR EXISTING DATA, SO I'VE SENT MR. KRAY TO COLLECT DISC COPIES OF EVERYTHING YOU HAVE, FOR PERSONAL DELIVERY TO OUR LABS.

I KNOW WHAT YOU'RE THINKING-- BUT RELAX, HE'S THE BEST OPERATIVE WE'VE GOT.

YOU HAVE HIM TO THANK FOR THAT GEL THAT REDUCES ALIEN BLOOD TO THE pH OF WATER. TOOK IT RIGHT OUT FROM UNDER THE GRANT CORPORATION'S NOSE.

HE ALSO SCORED US THE SPECS FOR THOSE TASER-WEB LAUNCHERS. THERE'S NO ONE ELSE I'D TRUST ON THIS MISSION.

WHAT CONCERNS ME MOST IS HOW THEY UNSCRAMBLED THE SIGNAL. THEY DIDN'T HACK THE CODES, THEY JUST WALKED RIGHT IN.

NOW INTERNATIONAL SECURITY'S ON THE CASE, AND EVERYONE'S SCARED OF THEIR OWN SHADOW.

IT'S GOING TO BE A BAD TIME, ERNST. I ENVY YOU OUT THERE ON YOUR ISLAND. WE COULD ALL DO WITH A LITTLE PEACE AND SECURITY RIGHT NOW.

INDEED.

MESSAGE ENDS

I GREW A SET OF "DUMMIES"-- CLONED BODY TISSUE DESIGNED TO MIMIC LIVING MATTER-- FOR IMPLANTATION AND GESTATION.

THE ALIEN HAS INSPIRED MANY NEW COMMODITIES...

...BUT WHAT IF THE CREATURE ITSELF COULD BE ADAPTED-- BIOENGINEERED TO BECOME MAN'S TOOL INSTEAD OF HIS ADVERSARY?

CONSUMER BIOLOGICALS?

EXACTLY! BUT WITH THEIR INNATE HOSTILITY REMOVED BY SPLICING THEIR D.N.A. WITH THAT OF MORE PASSIVE, LESS PREDATORY CREATURES.

RESTRICTED

I EXCLUDED ALL THE MAJOR CARNIVORES AND PRIMATES. THE BEST TEST RESULTS WERE WITH DOMESTICS: SHEEP, LAMAS, SOME CATTLE.

OF COURSE, THERE WERE A FEW SETBACKS.

I NURTURED THEM, SCULPTED THEIR GENES, CRAFTED THEIR FLESH INTO NEW VEHICLES OF MORTALITY... YET STILL THEY REFUSED MY GIFTS.

ARE ALL CHILDREN SO UNGRATEFUL?

SIR, I...

THE QUEENS. THEY'RE THE ONES-- ALWAYS DEFYING ME, BUT I'LL BREAK THEM LIKE I DID THE OTHERS. HAVE THEM RUNNING TO HEEL LIKE THE BEASTS THEY ARE.

LAST NIGHT, I DREAMED I WAS BALANCED ON THE EDGE OF A VAST ABYSS, ITS FLOOR OBSCURED BY AN OCEAN OF GREY CLOUDS.

INSTEAD OF FOLLOWING THE SAFE PATH, I DELIBERATELY STEPPED OFF--INTO THE UNKNOWN.

A RATHER BLATANT METAPHOR, DON'T YOU AGREE?

I WOULDN'T KNOW. I NEVER DREAM.

OF COURSE NOT. I'M SORRY.

WHAT'S YOUR REPORT?

IT'S THE SUBJECT SIR. HE'S ON THE MOVE.

IT TOOK TWO THOUSAND CONVICTS TO HACK CHARON OUT OF THE ROCK AND ICE.

TWO THOUSAND MEN DIGGING THEIR OWN GRAVES.

PAULIE FINN IS A GRAVE ROBBER.

ON HIS DAYS OFF FROM THE KITCHENS, HE STEALS FROM THE DEAD TO SUPPLEMENT HIS LIVING.

A SIDELINE THAT COULD TURN THE STRONGEST STOMACHS.

BUT PAULIE IS A PRACTICAL MAN.

WORKING IN THE KITCHEN HAS GIVEN HIM A HEALTHY DISREGARD FOR DEAD MEAT.

MMWWAAAHH!!

WHAT THE CHRIST IS THIS?!

S'LIKE A GODDAMN MEATLOCKER...

GAAA!!

URGHH

IT'S THE LIVE ONES YOU HAVE TO WATCH OUT FOR.

AS A CHILD HE REMEMBERS BEING TERRIFIED OF THE DARK. IT WAS WHERE THE MONSTERS LIVED, PATIENT, PREDATORY. WAITING FOR THE CARELESS TRESPASSES OF THE UNWARY.

HE FINALLY OVERCAME HIS FEAR BY EMBRACING IT.

NOW HE RELISHES THE ANONYMITY OF THE SHADOWS-- STALKING THE TWILIGHT WORLD BETWEEN COMMERCE AND CRIME.

A SILENT HUNTER.

THERE ARE STILL MONSTERS IN THE DARKNESS-- SOME OF THEM ARE HUMAN.

IS THIS A PRIVATE MOMENT OF MOODY INTROSPECTION OR CAN ANYONE JOIN IT?

BY ALL MEANS, BE MY GUEST.

SEEMS LIKE WE'RE THE ONLY ONES WHO ENJOY THE VIEW?

I LIKE TO COME HERE SOMETIMES, AWAY FROM THE GRUNTS AN' GREASERS. JUST ME AND THE UNIVERSE-- HELPS PUT THINGS INTO PERSPECTIVE.

HOW'S THAT?

WELL, WE MAY BE THE SMARTEST MONKEYS ON THE ROCK, BUT OUT HERE THAT DON'T MEAN JACK SHIT.

I THINK I KNOW WHAT'S UPSET HIM.

YOU MURDERED ONE OF MY MEN, YOU BASTARD! KILLED HIM AND TRY TO CALL IT JUSTICE!!

AS YOU WITNESSED, CORPORAL CHOI DELIBERATELY DESTROYED AN EXPENSIVE SPECIMEN.

HE COULD EASILY HAVE SUBDUED IT WITH A TASER BUT CHOSE NOT TO. A CONSCIOUS ACT OF SABOTAGE.

WHAT!

AS DIRECTOR OF THIS FACILITY, I FELT OBLIGED TO AUTHORIZE THE MAXIMUM PENALTY.

MY GOD! HE WAS RIGHT! YOU ARE OUT OF YOUR MIND!!

THIS IS A SCIENTIFIC RESEARCH ESTABLISHMENT, NOT A MILITARY OUTPOST. YOU'RE UNDER MY JURISDICTION, FOLLOWING MY ORDERS!

WE'RE MARINES! NOT LAB RATS! I CAME HERE WITH A FULL PLATOON-- I'VE A HANDFUL LEFT BECAUSE OF YOU!!

I'M TIRED OF YOUR MEN'S INSUBORDINATION AND LOCKER ROOM MENTALITY. AS OF NOW, MR. LARSON WILL RELIEVE YOU OF ALL DUTIES.

GRACE WILL ARRANGE FOR YOU AND YOUR MEN'S IMMEDIATE RETURN TO EARTH.

YOU'RE AN IRRITATION I'M NO LONGER PREPARED TO ENDURE.

NOW IF YOU'LL EXCUSE ME...

...MR. LARSON AND I HAVE BUSINESS TO ATTEND TO.

THERE! LOOK! DO YOU SEE IT?

SEE WHAT? I... MY GOD, IS THAT... A TATTOO?

MEET BILLY SINCLAIR, AN OLD BUDDY OF MINE. I WAS WITH HIM WHEN HE GOT IT DONE ON SHORE LEAVE IN MELBOURNE TEN YEARS AGO.

HE SUPPOSEDLY DIED LAST MONTH. FAULTY AIRLOCK-- EXPLOSIVE DECOMPRESSION. THEY SHOULD'VE HAD TO SCRAPE HIM OFF THE WALLS, BUT THERE HE IS.

ALL UTENSILS TO BE LEFT IN THE WASH

THAT MEANS YOU TOO DEEGAN!!

TAPE'S FULL OF THEM. SOME I KNOW. OTHERS--IT'S HARD TO TELL.

QUESTION IS, JOHN, WHAT'RE YOU GOING TO DO ABOUT IT?

YOU DON'T KNOW WHAT YOU'RE ASKING.

I KNOW THIS. KLEIST'S A PSYCHO, AND HE'S GOT TO BE STOPPED! YOU HAVE TO LET THEM KNOW WHAT'S HAPPENING HERE!!

IT'S NOT THAT EASY.

DO YOU KNOW WHAT IT'S LIKE TO LIVE IN FEAR TWENTY-FOUR HOURS A DAY, EVERY DAY WITHOUT END?!

THIS PLACE IS A GULAG, SIX MONTHS COMMUNICATION TIME FROM EARTH. KLEIST CAN DO ANYTHING HE LIKES HERE--ANYTHING!

WE GET A LOT OF 'ACCIDENTS.' UNDERSTAND? NO ONE GOES HOME--EVER!

ONLY A FEW OF US KNOW THE TRUTH. WE KEEP A LOW PROFILE. MAKE TOO MANY WAVES, LARSON'S BOYS PAY YOU A SURPRISE VISIT, AND THAT'S IT...

YOU'RE GONE.

ANOTHER 'ACCIDENT.'

I WANT TO LIVE TO SEE MY KIDS AGAIN. I WON'T DIE ON THIS ROCK. I'M RISKING EVERYTHING TALKING TO YOU.

JOYCE, YOU'RE NOT THE ONLY ONE TAKING A RISK...

THERE'S SOMETHING YOU SHOULD KNOW.

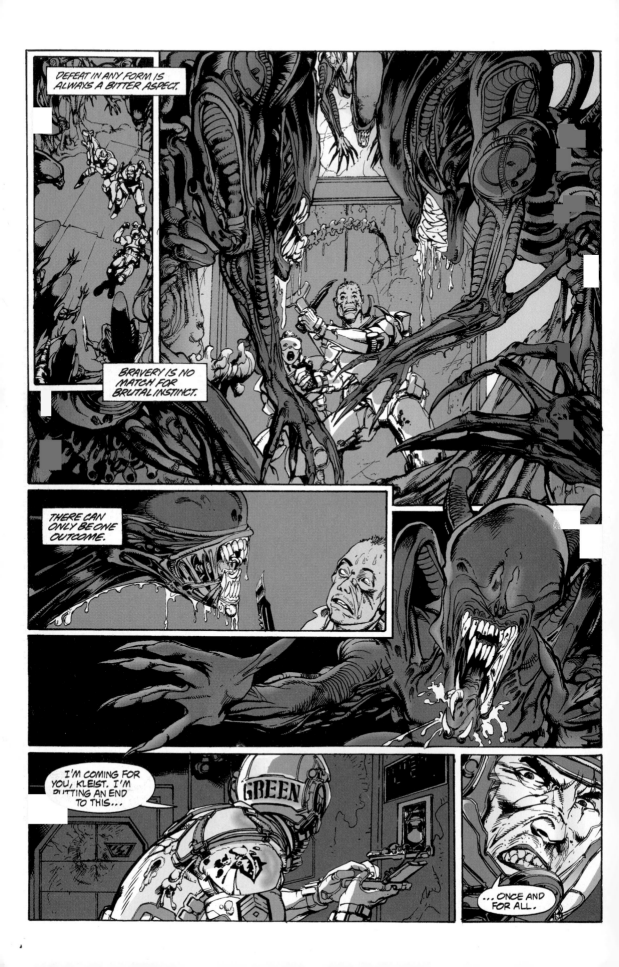

IT WAS AN AUDACIOUS PLAN, I ADMIRE THAT.

THE HOLO' OF OLD DESOUZA ESPECIALLY. HOPING TO MAKE ME SO PARANOID ABOUT INFILTRATION THAT I'D HAND YOU THE CHIMERA DATA WITHOUT A SECOND THOUGHT.

YOU MADE ONE FATAL ERROR: ALL ZCT OPERATIVES ABOVE GRADE NINE HAVE A SECURITY CODE SURFACE COATED ON THEIR RIGHT KIDNEY.

YOU, A SUPPOSED GRADE TWELVE, DID NOT.

UH?

THAT'S RIGHT. WE'VE KNOWN YOU WORKED FOR THE GRANT CORPORATION ALL ALONG.

LET YOU FEED US THE TASER AND PH GEL DATA--WE WANTED TO KNOW WHAT YOU WERE AFTER, WHO YOUR CONTACTS WERE.

WE'VE NETTED QUITE A HAUL THANKS TO YOU INCLUDING CAPTAIN PALMER.

NUH NUH NO. SHE'S NOT...

I MAY BE MAD AS THEY SAY I AM BUT I'M NOT STUPID! YOU WILL TELL ME EVERYTHING YOU KNOW...

OTHERWISE YOU'LL SOON DISCOVER THERE IS SUCH A THING AS A FATE WORSE THAN DEATH.

NOOHH!

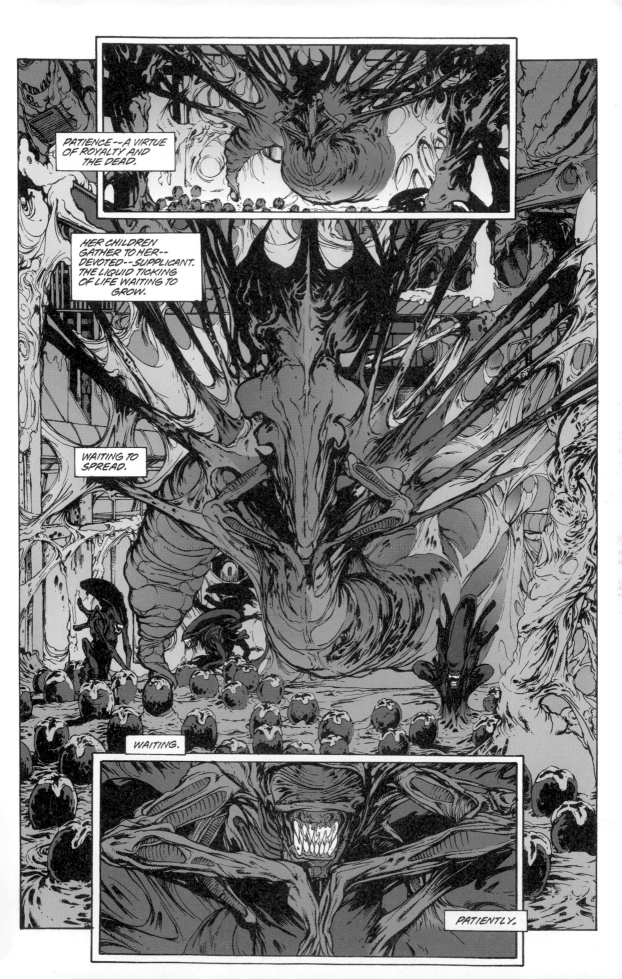

PATIENCE--A VIRTUE
OF ROYALTY AND
THE DEAD.

HER CHILDREN
GATHER TO HER--
DEVOTED--SUPPLICANT.
THE LIQUID TICKING
OF LIFE WAITING TO
GROW.

WAITING TO
SPREAD.

WAITING.

PATIENTLY.

CONTRARY TO OPINION, SCIENCE ISN'T ALWAYS A LINEAR PROFESSION. AN OCCUPATION OF THEORIES AND GOALS LACKING SOUL AND SPONTANEITY.

IT'S AN ART FORM, SUBJECT TO THE DEMANDS OF ENDURANCE, AND VAGARIES OF INSPIRATION.

EVEN SO, IT WAS AN UNEXPECTED IRONY THAT THE ONE WHO WOULD STEAL MY LIFE'S WORK SHOULD YIELD MY GREATEST TRIUMPH.

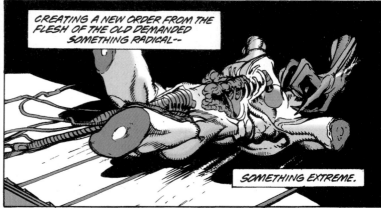

CREATING A NEW ORDER FROM THE FLESH OF THE OLD DEMANDED SOMETHING RADICAL--

SOMETHING EXTREME.

THIS IS UNKNOWN TERRITORY, WHERE THE LAWS OF NATURE AND SCIENCE HAVE YET TO BE DEFINED.

KICK IN THE FLOODS.

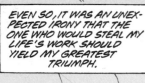

SUCCESS AFTER SO MANY MONTHS OF BITTER FAILURE? I CAN SCARCELY BELIEVE IT.

I HAVE DONE MANY QUESTIONABLE THINGS, BUT THIS--THIS WILL BE MY VINDICATION.

I TRIED EVERYTHING. PARASITIC BONDING VIRUSES -- CYBERNETIC IMPLANTS -- LIVE HUMAN HOSTS INSTEAD OF CLONED BODY MASS.

ALL USELESS.

I WAS MIRED IN MY OBSESSION TO CULTURE AN ALIEN QUEEN, BLIND TO OTHER OPTIONS.

IT TOOK THE INTRUSION OF KRAY--THE ROGUE ELEMENT, THE INVADER IN OUR MIDST-- TO INSPIRE WIDER BREADTH OF VISION.

GOOD EVENING, MR. KRAY.

I'M SO GLAD YOU COULD FIND THE TIME TO JOIN US.

ALLOW ME TO INTRODUCE THE LATEST ADDITION TO MY HAPPY BROOD... YOUR SON!

OH, GOD.

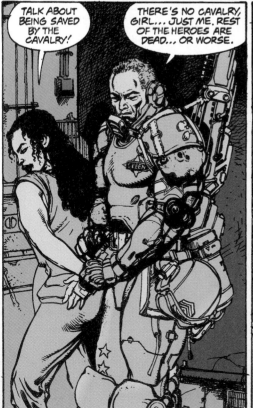

"MY JUDGMENT WAS INCORRECT."

"THE KING REFRAINED FROM ATTACKING KRAY, NOT BECAUSE ITS NATURAL SAVAGERY HAD BEEN BRED OUT, BUT BECAUSE KRAY WAS STRAPPED DOWN... INCAPACITATED..."

"KRAY WAS SPARED BECAUSE HE WASN'T PER-CEIVED AS A THREAT."

"UNLIKE NOW."

YET PERHAPS ALL IS NOT LOST.

IT'S ALL A MATTER OF PERSPECTIVE.

NOTHING. ALL FOR NOTHING.

THE WORK, THE LIVES-- ALL WASTED. CHRIST, THEY FED ME AS MUCH ROPE AS I WANTED AND WATCHED ME HANG MYSELF WITH IT.

YOU OKAY?

HM? YEAH, I'M FINE.

OLD ACCESS TUNNELS. JOINT'S RIDDLED WITH THEM. BACK FROM WHEN THIS WAS A PENAL COLONY. FEWER CAMERAS DOWN HERE.

CAN WE REACH YOUR SHIP THIS WAY?

NOT ENTIRELY, BUT CLOSE ENOUGH. I NEED DEEGAN, THOUGH. A GOOD CAPTAIN DOESN'T DESERT HER CREW.

I APPRECIATE THE RISK YOU TOOK COMING FOR ME.

FORGET IT, I WAS IN THE NEIGHBORHOOD ANYWAY. BESIDES, I OWED YOU ONE FOR CALLING YOU A COMPANY STOOGE.

YOU KNOW I'M AN AGENT FOR GRANT CORP, OR AT LEAST WAS UNTIL TODAY?

SO I HEARD. TO BE HONEST, AFTER ALL I'VE BEEN THROUGH, I COULDN'T GIVE A DAMN ANYMORE. I JUST WANT TO GET THE HELL OFF THIS ROCK.

I STOOD BY FOR TOO LONG, WATCHING KLEIST PLAY SOME SICK GAME WITH THE PEOPLE HERE.

NO ONE KNEW HIS GAME, SO NO ONE KNEW HIS RULES. YOU MAKE A WRONG MOVE, YOU DIE.

SOONER OR LATER SOMETHING HAD TO GIVE.

YOUR ARRIVAL WAS A KIND OF CATALYST FOR ME. IT WAS NOW OR NEVER. THE TRUTH HAD TO COME OUT OR I'D DIE HERE--NEVER SEE MY KIDS AGAIN.

SO YOU GAMBLED YOUR LIFE ON TALKING TO ME--A SPY?

YEAH, WELL, THINGS DIDN'T QUITE WORK OUT AS I'D PLANNED.

YOU AND ME BOTH.

AT LEAST WE'VE GOT OUR HEALTH.

YEAH, BUT FOR HOW LONG?

THAT'S WHAT I LIKE ABOUT YOU, JOHN, OR WHOEVER YOU ARE.

YOU'RE A PESSIMIST AFTER MY OWN HEART.

NOTHING.

I'M NOT REGISTERING A SINGLE TRACE. NOTHING'S MOVING DOWN HERE.

FASCINATING. I AT LEAST EXPECTED THERE TO BE AN INNER CADRE LEFT BEHIND TO PROTECT THE QUEEN.

THERE WAS.

THIS LOOKS LIKE WHAT'S LEFT OF THEM.

YES, YOU'RE RIGHT. SEE THE DIFFERENT CRANIAL CONFIGURATION... THE OVERSIZED MANDIBLES?

THIS WAS THE QUEEN'S ELITE. HER PRAETORIAN GUARD.

PROFESSOR, OVER HERE. I'VE GOT A TRACE.

TIK TIK TIK

LIGHTS ARE ON, BUT NO ONE'S HOME. KINDA REMINDS ME OF A GIRL I ONCE KNEW.

LOOKS LIKE THEY ALL TOOK OFF IN A HURRY.

MAYBE THEY DIDN'T HAVE A CHOICE.

WHICH WAY NOW?

FAR SIDE OF THE CHAMBER. AN ACCESS TUNNEL FEEDS DIRECTLY INTO THE HANGAR BAY.

WAIT! HEAR SOMETHING?

WHAT IS THAT?

SCREAMING. PEOPLE SCREAMING.

KEEP MOVING.

I'M DOWN TO MY LAST CLIP. IF WE HIT HEAVY RESISTANCE, IT'S GOING TO COME DOWN TO SOME HARD CHOICES. UNDERSTAND?

IF IT COMES TO THAT, I'LL DO US ALL, BUT HEY...

...WE'RE ALMOST HOME FREE--

KRAY!

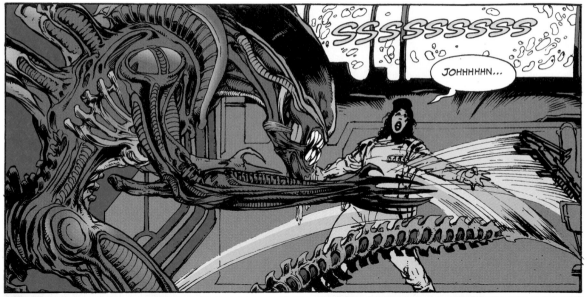

WE MAINTAINED ORBIT FOR THREE DAYS, MONITORING TRANS-MISSIONS, AND WATCHING FOR SURVIVORS,

THE ONLY THING WE PICKED UP WAS STATIC.

IN HINDSIGHT, OUR FAILURE WAS INEVITABLE. MANKIND'S PRIZED INTELLECT HAS BECOME OUR GREATEST CONCEIT.

WE DRESS OURSELVES IN TECHNOLOGY, AND THINK IT MAKES US OMNIPOTENT.

THE ALIEN FUNCTIONS ON A BASER, PURER LEVEL. ITS PURPOSE IS THE SIMPLEST...REPRODUCE AND SURVIVE.

WE CANNOT CONTROL THEM, OR CALL THEM EVIL...

...YET WE ALLOW MEN LIKE KLEIST TO ASSUME POWER.

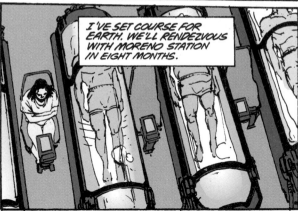

I'VE SET COURSE FOR EARTH. WE'LL RENDEZVOUS WITH MORENO STATION IN EIGHT MONTHS.

THIS IS CAPTAIN PALMER OF THE TRANSPORT VESSEL CALIBAN SIGNING OFF.

Biographies

Ian Edginton does not exist. He is in fact a collective pseudonym assumed by an infinite number of monkeys working at an infinite number of typewriters. Raised on diets of junk food and trash TV, they have been successfully working in the comics industry for the past nine years. For the purpose of conventions, they hired an actor to impersonate them, but he was fired after he got hammered on tequila slammers and ran around naked but for a strategically placed squirt of Cheez Whiz™. The monkeys have since moved to Los Angeles, and there is no truth to the rumor they are dating Anna Nicole Smith.

Will Simpson's clone sits in a room of wood, manacled to a drawing board, repeating "Rosebud" endlessly . . . while his comic-strip work — "Judge Dredd," "Tyrannasaurus Rex," and "Rogue Trooper" for 2000 A.D. — and comic-book work — *Aliens: Rogue* for Dark Horse and *Hellblazer, Vamps,* and *Batman: Legends of the Dark Knight* for DC Comics — continue to be re-packaged and earn money from all over the world. The real Simpson lounges around a lot in a sordid display of majestic splendor, reaping these rewards while painting other subjects he enjoys.

John Bolton spends far too much time painting in his eerie, prop-filled studio in North London. An award-winning artist who has worked on books with Chris Claremont, Neil Gaiman, Clive Barker, Sam Raimi, Anne Rice, and many others, and whose ethereal vampire-women and magical creatures have made his work much sought after, John has handled assignments for every major publisher in the comics field. His interest in the stylishly bizarre is evidenced throughout his work, and he currently has his own international fan club and magazine.

ALIENS ROGUE
GALLERY

In its eleven-year history, Dark Horse has worked with many great Aliens artists. The following gallery includes illustrations from Nelson, Will Simpson, Kent Williams, Christopher Scalf, Mike Mignola, Paul Johnson, Tim Bradstreet, and Guy Burwell.

This Nelson piece was the cover of the first collected edition of *Aliens: Rogue*.

Will Simpson cover art from issues 1, 2, and 4 of the *Aliens: Rogue* comic-book series.

Christopher Scalf cover art to the one-shot *Aliens* comic book *Aliens: Pig*.

Mike Mignola cover art from the spellbinding tale *Aliens: Salvation*.

Paul Johnson cover art from *Aliens: Sacrifice*, the 48-page *Aliens* tale written by Peter Milligan.